PREDATORS
LIONS

Sally Morgan

Belitha Press

LOOK FOR THE PREDATOR

Look for the lion in boxes like this.
Here you will find extra facts, stories
and other interesting information about lions.

First published in the UK in 2003 by

Belitha Press
A member of Chrysalis Books plc
64 Brewery Road, London N7 9NT

Design and editorial production
Bender Richardson White
Copyright © Belitha Press 2002

ISBN 1 84138 668 5

British Library Cataloguing in Publication Data for this book is available from the
British Library.

10 9 8 7 6 5 4 3 2 1

Acknowledgements
We wish to thank the following individuals and organizations for their help and
assistance and for supplying material in their collections:
CORBIS Corporation/Images: pages 1, 2, 3, 8, 8–9 top, 11 bottom, 12 bottom,
16–17 bottom, 19 bottom, 22, 29, 30; 4 bottom (Mary Ann McDonald); 4 top, 5, 20
bottom (Yann Arthus-Bertrand); 17 bottom (Gallo Images); 23 top (Kevin Schafer);
24 top (Hulton Deutsch Collection); 25 (Wolfgang Kaehler); 26 (Charles & Josette
Lenars); 27 (Richard T. Nowitz); 31 (Roger Tidman). Natural History Photo Agency:
pages 5, 10, 16 top (Stephen Krasemann); 14 (Andy Rouse); 9, 15 bottom (Martin
Harvey); 11 top (Nigel J. Dennis); 12 top, 20 top (Jonathan & Angela Scott): 13
(Steve Toon); 18 (Daryl Balfour); 19 top (Steve Robinson); 21, 24 bottom, 28
(Christophe Ratier); 23 bottom (Norbert Wu). Papilio: pages 6, 7 top (P. Marazzi);
15 top (Dennis Johnson); 17 top (John Farmar).

Editorial Manager: Joyce Bentley
Assistant Editor: Clare Chambers
Project Editor: Lionel Bender
Text Editor: Kate Phelps
Design and Make-up: Ben White
Picture Research: Cathy Stastny
Consultant: John Stidworthy

Printed in Hong Kong

◀ Lions have powerful
jaws and sharp teeth
for killing prey (see
page 12).

▶ A lioness stalks her
prey on the African
savanna (see page 16).

CONTENTS

KING OF THE BEASTS

The lion is often called the 'king of beasts' because of its size and power. Lions are predators, or hunters – they eat other animals. The animals they hunt are called prey. Another name for a predator is carnivore, or meat-eater.

Lions belong to a group of animals called mammals. All mammals have four limbs and most have a body covered in hair. The female mammal produces milk to feed her young. Lions are cats, and they are closely related to cheetahs, leopards, tigers and pet cats.

▲ Young mammals, such as these lion cubs, suck milk from their mother for the first few weeks of their life.

▼ The adult lions allow the cubs to play, but they get a warning if they get too close!

Lions are found mostly in Africa south of the Sahara Desert, where they live mainly on the flat grasslands known as savanna. They live together in a small group called a pride. Within a pride there will be one or two male lions, five or six female lions, or lionesses, and their young. The young lions range in age from newborn to one or two years of age.

ONE TYPE OF LION
There is only one species of lion and its proper scientific name is *Panthera leo*. Most lions live in Africa, but a few live in northwestern India.

▼ Once the lionesses have caught their prey, the other members of the pride come to feed.

KILLING MACHINE

A lion is a fearsome animal. It has a large and powerful body that ripples with muscles. The male lion's job is to defend the pride, while the female is the hunter.

The body of the lion is perfectly designed for hunting and killing prey. The powerful body is strong enough to catch and hold on to prey and heavy enough to pull large prey, such as zebras and wildebeests, down to the ground. Lions cannot run for long distances. Instead, they run for a short distance at speeds of between 40 and 50 km/h. They can leap too – as far as 9m.

BIG CAT

An adult male lion is 2.7 m long from nose to tail and stands about 1.2 m high at the shoulder. He weighs between 150 and 250 kg.

◀ The large canine teeth at the corner of the mouth are curved so they can stab and grip prey.

▲ It is easy to tell the male and female lion apart. The male lion is larger and has a thick mane surrounding his face and covering the neck, shoulders and chest.

The male lion is larger than the lioness. His thick mane of hair makes him look even larger and much fiercer. The mane starts to grow when the lion is about two years old and continues to get thicker throughout his life. Male lions are designed for fighting, so their mane protects their head and shoulders. The lioness is much lighter and, although she is not as powerful, she is better suited to hunting.

▶ This lioness needs all her strength to pull down this prey. She will grip the animal with her claws and teeth.

GRASSLAND HOME

The savanna grasslands of Africa are home to herds of grazing animals such as antelopes, wildebeests and zebras. These animals attract predators such as lions, cheetahs and leopards.

For much of the year, the weather is hot and dry. The savanna turns golden brown during the dry months. As water becomes scarcer, herds of grazing animals move nearer to water holes and rivers where they can find water each day. The savanna looks very different during the rainy seasons. Once the rains have come, the grasses produce fresh growth, and the savanna is green again.

▼ A herd of zebra graze on the savanna. Most of the savanna is flat with a few flat-topped acacia trees which provide shade during the long, hot summer.

THE SERENGETI
The Serengeti is a large area of savanna in Tanzania. During certain times of year, millions of wildebeest and zebra move across the plains in search of fresh grass. The huge number of animals means that there is plenty of food for lions and other predators.

Each pride of lion has a territory, or range, in which it lives. The territory has to provide the lions with all the food and water that they require. Territories vary in size from 20 to 400 sq km, depending on the size of the pride and the amount of food available. The male lions patrol the boundaries of the territory. They mark trees and boulders with urine. Other lions will smell the urine and know that they are trespassing. The males of neighbouring prides may fight if they meet each other.

▲ This herd of buffalo includes a mother and her calf. The animals stay in a herd to protect one another against predators such as lions. They are just one of the many types of grazing animal found on the savanna.

▶ A Thomson's gazelle mother and calf. On the savanna, grazing animals tend to give birth at the same time of year – after the rains, when the grass and trees burst into growth.

LION FOOD

The favourite prey animals of the lion include antelopes, gazelles, zebras, wildebeests and their calves, but they will eat small mammals, birds and eggs. When they are hungry, lions will eat almost any other animal.

▼ This lioness has caught a warthog and is carrying it back to the rest of the pride.

A zebra or wildebeest is large enough to feed the whole pride. However, lionesses do not catch large prey everyday, so they feed on smaller animals such as mongooses, impalas, dik-diks, warthogs and even porcupines. When food is scarce they will feed on insects, fish, small birds, snakes and eggs. When lions are very hungry, they scavenge on the remains of dead animals.

DAILY MEAT

Lions eat between 5 and 7 kg of meat per day, but when there is plenty of food around, a lion may gorge on as much as 30 kg of meat in a single day. Then it may go days without eating.

Wildebeests and their calves are favourite foods of the lion. Lone male lions prey on the calves as they are easy for one lion to kill on its own. Lionesses, hunting together, will prey on the adults and calves.

The hartebeest is a grazing animal that is found in small herds on the savanna.

Lions are thieves too. If the opportunity arises, they will steal food from other predators. Running after prey uses a lot of energy and there is a risk of injury. It is much easier to steal food from others. As much as half of a lion's food may be taken from predators such as leopards, cheetahs and hyenas.

Hunting and chasing prey is very tiring. Once a lion has eaten as much as it wants, it will spend the rest of the day sleeping or resting in the shade of acacia trees. Lions may rest for up to 20 hours every day.

MIGHTY WEAPONS

The lion's main weapons are its claws and teeth. The claws are used to grip prey while the sharp teeth are used to kill and to rip the victim's body apart.

A lion's claws are curved, sharp and up to 8 cm long. They are extremely strong and are ideal for holding on to prey. Just like a pet cat, the claws of a lion can be pulled into the paws when they are not in use. This prevents them from being damaged or worn down. Also it helps a lion to walk silently on the pads of its paws. If a claw is lost, a new one grows in its place.

▲ A lion has four toes on its back legs and five on its front. Beneath each toe is a pad which acts as a cushion and helps to soften any noise as it approaches prey.

▶ The lion has strong jaws that can lock around the neck of its prey and suffocate it. It uses the weight of its body to stop the animal from struggling.

The short pointed teeth at the front of the mouth are called incisors. They are used to grip prey. Next to these are four extra-long curved teeth called canines. The molar teeth behind the canines have razor-sharp edges and are used to crush bone. These teeth can slice through tough skin and muscle. Lions do not chew their food. Instead, they bite off a large mouthful of meat and swallow it whole.

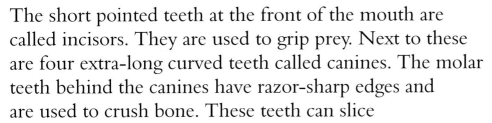 The lion has 30 teeth. The canines stick out because they are longer and larger than the incisors. They are used to stab prey.

ROUGH TONGUE

Lions have a tongue that is like rough sandpaper. This helps to grip prey. It is also good for pulling bits of meat off bones.

LION SENSES

Senses are just as important to a lion as its claws and teeth. Lions use their sense of sight, smell and hearing to locate their prey, especially when they are hunting at night.

The eyes of lions are excellent at detecting movement. Many animals remain perfectly still when they see a predator, rather than running away. By remaining still, the prey is less likely to be seen by the lion.

RUBBING HEADS

Lions need to be able to identify members of the pride when they return after hunting. Lions greet each other by rubbing their heads together. This releases a smell that others will recognize.

▼ Lions have two forward-pointing eyes that give them good 3-D (three-dimensional) vision. This helps them to judge distances.

Lions have good night vision and often hunt at night. The black spot in the middle of each eye is called the pupil. The pupils control how much light enters the eyes. In bright light, the pupils are small. In the dark, they open very wide to let in as much light as possible so that the lion can see well enough to be able to catch prey.

A good sense of hearing helps when hunting at night. Lions turn their head in the direction of a sound in order to hear better. The sound of a lion roaring can travel over many kilometres. A lion uses its roar to stay in touch with other members of the pride and to advertise its presence to other lions.

▲ The eyes of the lion are the largest of all the carnivores in the world. Lion cubs are born with eyes that are pale blue in colour, but the colour changes to amber as they grow older.

▼ A lioness lies on a rock from where she can watch the grazing animals on the savanna.

GOING HUNTING

In the pride, it is the job of the lioness to hunt for food. Unlike other large cats, lionesses often hunt in groups. By working together, there is a greater chance of success, and they can kill larger prey that will provide food for several days.

Lionesses cannot chase prey over long distances, so they try to get as close as possible before they start to run. A lioness will creep slowly towards her prey, keeping low on the ground so she is hidden in the grass. Each paw is placed down silently. She may stop and listen to check that she has not startled her prey. This slow approach can last as long as 30 minutes. Once she is close enough, she will pounce or rush at top speed towards her prey.

▼A lioness will approach her prey very slowly, creeping through the grass until she is within striking distance.

▲ Lions watch their prey from a high point, such as a hill or rock outcrop, before deciding on the best approach.

When lionesses hunt together, they may spread out in a fan around the prey. Then they slowly approach their victim from several directions at the same time. Another method involves one or two lionesses running towards the prey and driving it into other lionesses who are lying in ambush. Some of the biggest prey animals, such as large buffalos, can only be brought down by several lionesses working together.

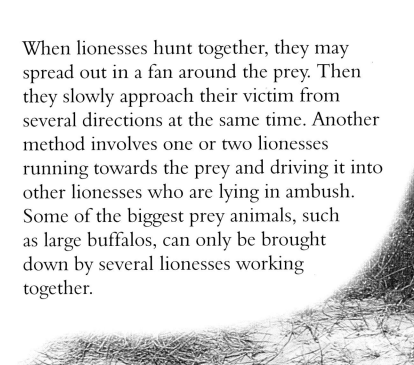

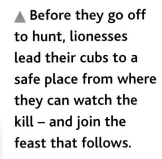

▲ Before they go off to hunt, lionesses lead their cubs to a safe place from where they can watch the kill – and join the feast that follows.

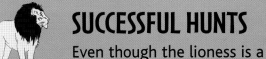

SUCCESSFUL HUNTS

Even though the lioness is a skilful hunter, only one hunt in five will end with a kill. Her prey often outrun her or see or hear her before she gets close enough to attack.

IN FOR THE KILL

Once a lioness has caught her prey, she has to kill it. She uses her strong jaws and sharp teeth as her main instruments of death.

▼ A lioness has started to chase her chosen prey and all the other antelopes and zebras are galloping to safety.

STARVING CUBS

When food is short, many lion cubs will starve to death as the adults will not leave enough food for them. The adults seem more concerned with their own survival – if their cubs die, they will mate again and have new cubs.

18

Lions kill their prey by suffocating them. A single lioness will grab the animal by the throat and crush its windpipe so that it cannot breathe. Sometimes she will bite the animal over its mouth to stop it from breathing. Within a few minutes the animal will be dead. When several lionesses make a kill, one of them will grip the neck and suffocate the animal, while the others stop the animal from struggling.

As soon as the prey has been killed, the rest of the pride arrives to feed. Although the lionesses have made the kill, it is the male lions that eat first. Once the male lions have eaten as much as they want, the lionesses can eat. The cubs are the last to feed. Often, they have to make do with the leftovers.

▲ A warthog will not provide much food for four lionesses.

▼ A lion will often steal a lioness's kill and feed on it first.

LEARNING TO KILL

Lion cubs have to learn to hunt. For the first year or two, young lions eat food that their mothers have killed. But they watch and learn and gradually get better at hunting.

A lion cub weighs about 2 kg when it is born, and for the first few months the mother stays close and feeds it milk. Young lion cubs stay hidden in a den when the lioness goes off to hunt. When they are two months old, they are introduced to the rest of the pride. Lion cubs of a similar age stay together in a nursery group. They are looked after by all the lionesses, not just their mother.

▲ The rough and tumble of play helps lion cubs to become expert hunters.

▶ Cubs play with the adult lions too. By playing, they learn some of the rules of the pride. If they break the rules, an adult will give them a slap.

Once they are large enough, their mothers will lead them to a kill where they can eat meat. Lion cubs love to play with each other. Play helps them to develop many of their hunting skills. They wrestle, tumble and practise stalking each other.

STRUGGLE FOR SURVIVAL

Lion cubs rely on their mother for food for the first year-and-a-half of their life. As many as one in four lion cubs die before they are one year old, either from starvation or because they are preyed on by hyenas and leopards.

When the cubs are about one year old, they follow their mother on a hunt. First, they are only allowed to watch, but later they are allowed to take part. They start hunting small animals and will not try to kill larger animals until they are about two years old.

▲ Lion cubs will be led to a kill by their mother, but they have to wait until all the adults have eaten before they can feed.

ENEMIES AND FIGHTS

A lion has few enemies. However, there are some animals that will dare to challenge a lion at a kill. For a male lion, one of the biggest threats comes from other male lions.

The lion's main enemy is the hyena. Lions and hyenas hunt the same types of animals, so they often compete with each other. Fights over food are common. A group of hyenas will gather around a lion kill waiting for an opportunity to steal meat. But lions are just as likely to scare hyenas away from their kills too.

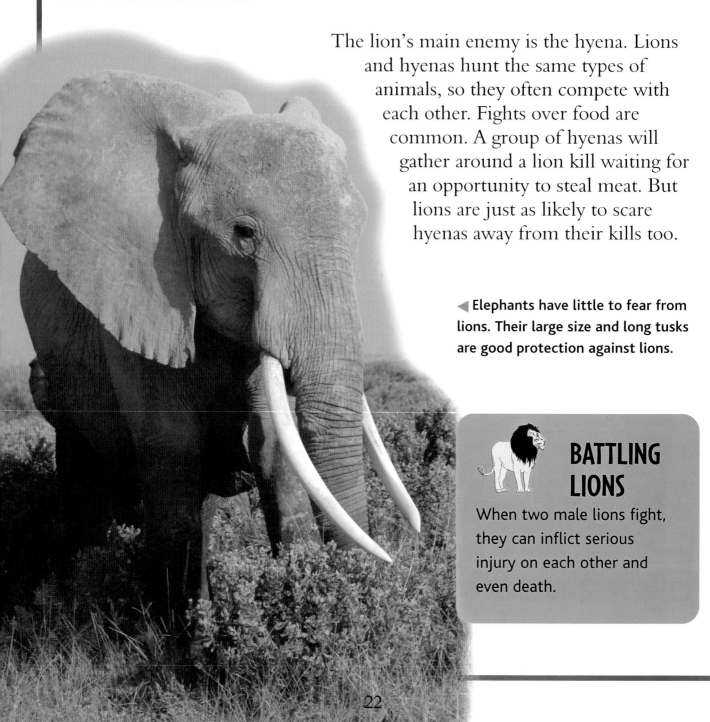

◀ Elephants have little to fear from lions. Their large size and long tusks are good protection against lions.

BATTLING LIONS

When two male lions fight, they can inflict serious injury on each other and even death.

A mother cheetah and her cubs feed on a kill. Cheetahs are smaller than lions. If a lion comes across this kill, it will chase the cheetahs away

Young lionesses stay with the pride, but it is very different for their brothers. Young males are chased away from the pride. Some will wander around on their own, but most join up with their brothers or cousins to form a small group. Together, they can find food more easily. Eventually, when they are fully grown, they try to take over a pride by challenging a male lion to a fight. The winner will live with the pride, while the loser is chased away. Older males or sick males may be too weak to lead a pride, and they give way to younger and fitter males.

Hyenas soon arrive at a kill, and they will lurk nearby, waiting for a chance to steal some meat.

UNDER THREAT

Once lions were shot by people on big game hunts. Now they are shot when they stray on to farmland or venture too close to people and livestock. But the greatest threat comes from the loss of habitat and from disease.

In Africa, there are large game reserves that give protection to all the animals living on the savanna. But this is not enough. In Africa, the human population is expanding rapidly and more land is being used to grow crops and to graze cattle, sheep and goats. This means that lion habitat is disappearing.

▲ At the turn of the twentieth century, big game hunting was popular. Nowadays most lions are protected, but in a few countries, this hunting is still allowed.

◀ Researchers studying the spread of canine distemper in lions have tranquillized two lionesses that are suffering from the disease.

Disease is also threatening lions. Pet dogs get a disease called distemper which can kill. The dogs pass the disease on to hyenas and the hyenas pass it on to lions. In the Serengeti Game Reserve in Tanzania, the disease has killed more than 1000 lions – that's one in three of all the lions in the Serengeti. Research is underway to see if the pet dogs can be vaccinated against the disease to stop it spreading any further.

▼ Many tourists visit game reserves in East Africa to see lions. Tourism brings a lot of money into the region, some of which goes into animal conservation.

THE ASIATIC LION

The Asiatic lion is an endangered species, which is found only in a small forested area of India. Fortunately the lion population is healthy, and there are plans to reintroduce lions into other forests. It is possible that Asiatic lions bred in zoos may be reintroduced to the wild.

LION FACTS

ANCIENT LIONS

About 10 000 years ago, huge lions roamed parts of Europe, the Middle East and the Americas. Although these lions no longer exist, their fierce reputation has lived on in legends, myths and folk stories.

BEASTLY WARS

Two thousand years ago, Roman crowds used to watch prisoners and wild beasts, such as lions, fighting to the death as a form of entertainment.

HEART OF A LION

In the Middle Ages, King Richard I of England was nicknamed 'the Lionheart' because of his strength and courage. He led armies to fight in the Middle East, where lions were often encountered.

LION MEDICINE

Many people believe that lions have supernatural powers. They believe that eating lion parts can restore lost power, cure illness and prevent death.

 A golden lion stands guard at the entrance to a Buddhist temple. Buddhists believe that the lion is a symbol of power.

MOTHER LOVE

A lioness living in Kenya adopted a baby oryx (a type of large antelope). Park rangers decided to rescue the baby oryx as the lioness could not feed her. Within a few months, she had found and adopted another oryx.

KING LION

Some African tribes believe that when important people in their tribe die, they are reborn as lions. In 1898, two lions killed many railway workers who were building the Uganda-Kenya railway. The workers refused to work, and all construction stopped. Local people believed that these lions were an ancient king and queen who had returned from the dead.

BORN FREE

One of the most famous lions of recent times was a lioness called Elsa. Her mother was killed, and she was rescued as a cub by Joy Adamson. She reared Elsa and released her back into the wild. The story of Elsa was featured in the film *Born Free* starring Virginia McKenna and Bill Travers.

▼ This ancient stone carving shows a lion killing a wildebeest.

27

LION WORDS

This glossary explains some of the words used in this book that you might not have seen before.

Ambush
to lie in wait.

Canine
large pointed tooth at the side of the mouth. A lion has four canines, two on the top jaw and two on the lower jaw.

Carnivore
an animal that hunts and eats other animals. Lions, cheetahs and tigers are carnivores.

Habitat
the place where an animal or plant lives, for example a savanna or a rainforest.

Incisor
the small pointed teeth at the front of the jaw.

Mammal
an animal that produces milk for its young. Mammals have varying amounts of hair on their bodies.

Molar
a large tooth near the back of the mouth used to crush food.

Patrol
to protect an area by walking up and down the boundaries.

▼ All mammals, including lions, produce milk for their young.

Predator

an animal that hunts other animals and eats them.

Prey

an animal that is hunted and killed by another animal – a predator – for food.

Pride

a group of lions that live together. A pride is made up of one or two adult males, several females and a group of youngsters.

Savanna

tropical grasslands, where there are dry seasons and rainy seasons.

Scavenger

an animal that feeds on dead and decayed bodies of animals.

Stalk

to creep up on something without being seen.

Supernatural

magical or mystical, something beyond the force of nature.

Territory

the area of land in which an individual or group of individuals lives.

Tranquillized

given a drug that makes an animal go to sleep for a short while.

Vaccinate

to inject an animal or a person with a drug that gives them protection against a certain disease.

Water hole

a pool of water to which animals come to drink, especially during the dry season.

▼ A lioness drinking water at the edge of a water hole.

LION PROJECTS

If you want to find out more about lions, here are some ideas for projects.

WATCHING LIONS

Not everyone can see lions in the wild, but you may be able to visit a zoo or an animal park which keeps lions. Imagine you are studying lions. Take a notebook with you and make notes of what you observe. For example, watch where the lions walk and where they urinate or sharpen their claws. What do they do when they walk past each other? Do they sniff each other or rub heads? Study the differences between the males and females. Then compare how lions behave with other predators you can see at the zoo.

WHAT EATS WHAT?

Starting with lions, draw a food chain for wildlife on the Serengeti grasslands of East Africa. A food chain is a diagram linking each animal with the animals or plants it feeds on. The text in this book will give you some of the 'links' in the lions' chain. To find more links, look at other books in your local library or look at some of the Internet sites listed opposite. See how many links you can make. Do any other African predators have similar animals and plants in their food chains? Are these predators competing with lions for food?

◀ Male and female lions look very different. The lioness has a slim, muscular body which is suited to hunting. The male lion has a heavier body, and his mane protects his head and neck during fights with other males.

An Asiatic lioness. The Asiatic lion is smaller than the African lion, and the mane is shorter and does not cover the ears.

PAW PRINTS

Lion tracks (footprints) can tell a field researcher where the animal travelled from and where it went. Trackers can tell how heavy the animal is and whether it is male or female, young or old, healthy or injured. You may not be able to track lions, but in muddy and sandy ground you could follow the tracks of other mammals such as deer, foxes, squirrels, or pet cats and dogs. Compare the numbers of toes and the size of the tracks.

HOW YOU CAN HELP

In the wild, lions are under threat. You can help protect them by supporting one of the many wildlife organizations that study lions and ensure their habitats are not destroyed.

LIONS ON THE WEB

If you have access to the Internet, try looking up these websites:

Enkosini Reserve
www.enkosini.com
This website is about the work of the Enkosini Reserve in South Africa, which is dedicated to the conservation of predators, especially lions.

Lion Research Centre
w1.adhost.com/lionresearch/main.html
A website with plenty of factual information about lion behaviour and research. Here, you can listen to recordings of the lion's roar.

Asiatic Lion Conservation
www.asiatic-lion.org
This website focuses on the Asiatic lion. Here you will find lot of information on this lion and how it is being conserved.

Born Free Foundation
www.bornfree.org.uk
The Born Free Foundation is an international wildlife charity which aims to prevent cruelty and suffering to animals, especially zoo animals. It was set up by Virginia McKenna and Bill Travers who starred in the film Born Free.

INDEX